My Story My Divorce God's Promise

My Story My Divorce God's Promise

~ THE BEGINNING ~

Corrie,

In all the twists & turns of this life, both good & not so good, we can count on God's promise

"I will never leave you or forsake you"

Prayers & Blessings to you & your family.

Kathiey V

July 2017

KathieyV

Dedication

To all those who took the time to help me through the most difficult time in my life. To my friends who prayed for me, cried with me, and took the time to love me in my grief. To my coworkers, my boss, and my neighbors. To all the professionals— my lawyer and her wonderful staff, my doctor, the private investigator and all of his associates, my banker, and the digital forensics team. To all of you who helped me discover the truth. To God, my one constant in this life. A deep, heartfelt thank-you for giving me hope, and through that hope, saving my life.

Table of Contents

Introduction

Being a pastor's wife for nearly twenty years, I thought I understood the emotions of a woman going through a separation and divorce. I now know this was extremely shortsighted of me. I had no idea. There was no way I could understand the deep pain and betrayal these women faced. I could not begin to realize the emotional turmoil and physical toll they would have to endure. The unwanted division of a family, the broken promises to love and to cherish, a vow to God cast aside as though meaningless. No, I could not grasp their gut-wrenching despair, not until now. Now that their experiences have become my reality. Now that my husband of thirty-seven years—the man I trusted with my life and my future—decided to do the same to me.

This book was written for anyone who wants to get a glimpse into the mind and emotions of a woman in the early days of the devastation of an unwanted separation and pending divorce. This is my attempt to express the raw emotion as I try to wrap my mind around this new path that has been chosen for me. I quote the scripture that helped me survive each day. I speak of the importance of friendship, faith, and of the hope and strength that can be found in God's word. I use my photography to display the assurance that God's beauty surrounds us even in our pain.

The Beginning

Frozen

Today I am frozen no story to tell.

I am lost in my sorrow, my personal hell

My thoughts are all jumbled as I try hard to pray.

I can't form a sentence, "Help" is all I can say.

Then comes to my mind a promise God made.

His Spirit is with me and comes to my aid

He is part of my soul and helps me to be heard,

with groans to my Father that are too deep for words.

KathieyV

Divorce—what an ugly word. I now find myself having to say this word, having to face its reality. I have experienced loss through death, having lost my parents and my little brother only a few short years ago. It was painful, and the grieving process was hard, but this is far different. It is like a death, but with intent. This was done by choice, but not my choice. No, our marriage was not perfect. I am not perfect, but I would have never considered doing this to my family. This divorce has no merit. There has been no infidelity or lack of caring, at least not on my part. In my opinion it is a selfish act and will have painful consequences for years to come. Somehow I must move on. But how? After thirty-seven years of marriage, I don't know where to start. Where can I turn but to God.

It was a normal Tuesday, or so I thought. I went to work, made it through the day, and looked forward to a relaxing evening at home. The plan was to take my dog for a walk, prepare a quick and simple meal, and then watch a little TV before going to bed to read. These plans were soon forgotten when I picked up the mail and found myself blindsided. My husband had been seeing a divorce attorney without my knowledge. He had filed for legal separation without a word to me. I had no idea my life was headed down this path. All I could think about was the effect this would have on my family and the pain this would cause everyone involved.

I didn't want this. This was not my choice.
Where can I turn but to God.

God is our refuge and strength, a very present help in trouble.
—Psalm 46:1

Father, in this extremely difficult time, help me remember
your promise.

"I will never leave you or forsake you."

This is not only emotional—it is physical. The emotional aspects of abandonment are gut wrenching. The physical aspects, I guess, follow a normal progression. My chest hurts. I feel as though I can't breathe. When I close my eyes, I see waves of darkness. My body burns, and there is an empty pit that inhabits my soul.

I didn't want this. This was not my choice.
Where can I turn but to God.

You Lord are my lamp:
the Lord turns my darkness into light.
—2 Samuel 22:29

Father, in this extremely difficult time, help me remember
your promise.

"I will never leave you or forsake you."

I picked up my grandson at daycare today—so precious, so innocent. I hate that he will no longer be able to come to Nana and Papa's house for stability and safety. A part of me died again at the unnecessary pain that this awfulness will cause and the weak example being set for him. I quickly texted my husband and said, "Are you sure you want to do this to our family?" He answered quickly and with resolve: "This is happening!"

I didn't want this division in our family. This was not my choice.
Where can I turn but to God.

Don't be afraid for I am with you. Don't be discouraged
for I am your God. I will strengthen you and help you.
I will hold you up with my victorious right hand.
—Isaiah 41:10

Father, in this extremely difficult time, help me remember
your promise.

"I will never leave you or forsake you."

He tells me he wants to remain friends. That he loves me, and he will always care for me. I guess in his mind taking care of me means that I will have very little while he enjoys his security. A friend does not do that to a friend.

I didn't want this. This was not my choice.
Where can I turn but to God.

Give your worries to the Lord, and he will care for you.
He will never let those who are good be defeated.
—Psalm 55:22

Father, in this extremely difficult time, help me remember
your promise.

"I will never leave you or forsake you."

Have you ever wanted to live and die all at the same time? I find myself wanting to leave this world and run into the arms of God. I have been leaning heavily on a song by a band called Casting Crowns. The song is titled "Praise You in This Storm." I listen to it every day and do my best to praise God during my storm. But the pain is so intense, and I feel so weak.

I didn't ask for this pain. This was not my choice.
Where can I turn but to God.

Be merciful to me, O God, be merciful, because I come
to you for safety. In the shadow of your wings I
find protection until the raging storms are over.
—Psalm 57:1

Father, in this extremely difficult time, help me remember
your promise.

"I will never leave you or forsake you."

I worry about my daughters. I hoped that they would think commitment was important and not to be taken lightly. If I can be cast off like I am nothing, thrown away after thirty-seven years of marriage, then a promise to God and a commitment to another must now mean very little in their eyes.

I didn't want these broken promises. This was not my choice.
Where can I turn but to God.

Let him have all your worries and cares, for he is always thinking about you and watching everything that concerns you.
—1 Peter 5:7

Father, in this extremely difficult time, help me remember
your promise.

"I will never leave you or forsake you."

I lay in bed at night unable to sleep. My body trembles; my skin burns; my head throbs.

I didn't want this chaos in my life. This was not my choice.
Where can I turn but to God.

My health may fail, and my spirit may grow weak, but God remains
the strength of my heart; he is mine forever.
—Psalm 73:26

Father, in this extremely difficult time, help me remember
your promise.

"I will never leave you or forsake you."

At this point in my life, I had envisioned happiness—times filled with family dinners, family trips. My focus was my family. Now my life is filled with broken promises, shattered dreams, and despair.

I didn't want this. This was not my choice.
Where can I turn but to God.

I sought the Lord, and he answered me.
He delivered me from all my fears.
—Psalm 34:4

Father, in this extremely difficult time, help me remember
your promise.

"I will never leave you or forsake you."

I went to the grocery store, thinking that it would take my mind off all the pain and confusion. It did not. I found myself in the store aisle staring at a can of baked beans. I don't know how long I stood there in my emotional daze. The last time I was there I had stability in my life. I no longer have stability in my family or my finances.

I didn't ask for this. This was not my choice.
Where can I turn but to God.

I lift my eyes to the hills, where does my help come from?
My Help comes from the Lord the maker of heaven and earth.
—Psalm 121:1–2

Father, in this extremely difficult time, help me remember
your promise.

"I will never leave you or forsake you."

It was a bad day. I listened to my song, I prayed, I worried then I listened to my song and prayed again. The pain is so deep and seems to shatter my heart and soul. A severe storm was headed my way. The wind was picking up and the trees swaying. The rain and lightening were moving in. I sat on the back porch watching with my dog by my side. I was sobbing. I had a strong urge to go home to God. I got my umbrella went onto the patio and sat in the middle of the chaos and fervently prayed. "Please take me home God. Please send a lightening bolt to take me to your peace." The storm ended. I am still here.

I didn't ask for this. This was not my choice.
Where can I turn but to God.

"No, I will not abandon you or leave you as orphans (in the storm)
I will come to you"
—John 14:18

Father, in this extremely difficult time, help me remember
your promise.

"I will never leave you or forsake you."

26

I love photography. As I review some of the photos I have taken over the years, I see images of family gatherings, holiday excursions, and the many good times now gone. This causes even greater pain.

I didn't ask for this. This was not my choice.
Where can I turn but to God.

Blessed are those who mourn, for they will be comforted.
—Matthew 5:4

Father, in this extremely difficult time, help me remember
your promise.

"I will never leave you or forsake you."

I am told to take baby steps. To focus on only one day at a time and not to look ahead. This is harder than I could have imagined.

I didn't want this. This was not my choice.
Where can I turn but to God.

Do not be afraid or discouraged, for the Lord will
personally go ahead of you. He will be with you;
He will neither fail you or abandon you.
—Deuteronomy 31:8

Father, in this extremely difficult time, help me remember
your promise.

"I will never leave you or forsake you."

The fear, uncertainty, and sorrow that I feel is constant. You would think that sleep, when it comes, would bring relief. It doesn't. When sleep does come, its short lived. I awake with my jaw clenched and my knuckles white.

I didn't ask for this. This was not my choice.
Where can I turn but to God.

When I called to you for help, you answered me and gave me strength.
—Psalm 138:3

Father, in this extremely difficult time, help me remember
your promise.

"I will never leave you or forsake you."

My family was here today. They will leave soon, and I will be alone.

I didn't ask for this. This was not my choice.
Where can I turn but to God.

The Lord is your protector. The Lord stands by your side
Shading and protecting you.
—Psalm 121:5

Father, in this extremely difficult time, help me remember
your promise.

"I will never leave you or forsake you."

I sit in church feeling vulnerable and alone, even though I am surrounded by hundreds of people. My pain is hidden but surely there. The pastor said, "Letting go is the hardest part."

I didn't want this. This was not my choice.
Where can I turn but to God.

In the day of trouble I call upon you, for you answer me.
—Psalm 86:7

Father, in this extremely difficult time, help me remember
your promise.

"I will never leave you or forsake you."

I am told the best thing to do is to try to keep my routine. Tough to do, but today I thought I would try. I went out for a jog. I can usually clear my mind and focus on things I enjoy during a run, such as what adventures we can have as a family, trying new recipes, photography, and the hope of travel. Today my current life situation was the one thing on my mind. I was only aware of my headache, my heartache, and the nausea that never seems to subside. I have had a jogging routine for years. I may mix it up a bit for distance, but it usually stays the same. Today, for the first time in over twenty years, I deviated from my usual course. It didn't feel right. I didn't like it—the uncertainty of where I was, the loss of the familiar. A foreshadowing of my new life. This new direction in my life that had been forced upon me.

I didn't want this. This was not my choice.
Where can I turn but to God.

Trust in the Lord with all your heart; do not depend on
your own understanding. Seek His will in all you do,
and he will show you which path to take.
—Proverbs 3:5–6

Father, in this extremely difficult time, help me remember
your promise.

"I will never leave you or forsake you."

My head hurts. My thoughts are tangled. My days are a roller coaster of emotion. Reaching deep inside for comfort, I remember my mom's favorite verse: Psalm 23.

Mom, you know I didn't want this. This was not my choice.
Where can I turn but to God.

The Lord is my shepherd; I shall not want.
He makes me to lie down in green pastures;
He leads me beside the still waters. He restores my soul.
He leads me in the paths of righteousness for His name's sake.
Yea, though I walk through the valley of the shadow of death,
I will fear no evil; for you are with me;
your rod and staff they comfort me.
You prepare a table before me in the presence of my enemies;
you anoint my head with oil; my cup overflows.
Surely goodness and mercy shall follow me all the days of my life;
and I will dwell in the house of the Lord forever.
—Psalm 23

Father, in this extremely difficult time, help me remember
your promise.

"I will never leave you or forsake you."

I sit in the living room with my family. Everyone is here, including the one who divides us. It is as though there is a giant elephant in the room that everyone is choosing to ignore. Everyone acts as though nothing has changed. They are probably hoping nothing has changed, not wanting to give up on the good. They don't realize that inside I am dying. My world has changed.

I didn't ask for this. This was not my choice.
Where can I turn but to God.

When I am afraid, I will put my trust in you.
—Psalm 56:3

Father, in this extremely difficult time, help me remember
your promise.

"I will never leave you or forsake you."

I wake up trembling, covered in sweat. I ask myself, "What is happening?" Then I remember the source of my anguish. I don't know how to pray.

I didn't ask for this. This was not my choice.
Where can I turn but to God.

In the same way the Spirit also comes to help us, weak as we are.
For we do not know how we ought to pray; the Spirit Himself pleads with God for us in groans that words cannot express.
—Romans 8:26

Father, in this extremely difficult time, help me remember
your promise.

"I will never leave you or forsake you."

In my grief I remembered a movie I once saw. A young woman was in danger. The man who was supposed to protect her took off, only concerned only for himself. "He left me. He left me," she cried out in fear. Someone stronger (in my case, God) came to her and said, "That's not what I'm going to do." I cried out in fear too. "He left me. He left me." Broken promises to love and cherish. Broken vows to me and to God. Left alone.

I didn't ask for this. This was not my choice.
Where can I turn but to God.

Be strong and courageous. Do not be afraid or terrified because of them,
for the Lord your God goes with you; He will never leave you or forsake you.
—Deuteronomy 31:6

Father, in this extremely difficult time, help me remember
your promise.

"I will never leave you or forsake you."

Going through the heartache and sadness is exhausting in itself. Now I must continue to meet my old responsibilities while taking on all the new ones that confront me. As I get ready for work, I am physically shaking. I am overwhelmed. I don't know where to start.

I didn't want this. This was not my choice.
Where can I turn but to God.

But He said to me, "My grace is sufficient for you,
for my power is made perfect in weakness."
—2 Corinthians 12:9

Father, in this extremely difficult time, help me remember
your promise.

"I will never leave you or forsake you."

I had a strange dream last night. I can't remember dreaming since my literal nightmare began, probably because I rarely sleep. Last night I dreamt that my soon to be ex was resting comfortably in his bed, propped up casually, and happily reading his magazine. My girls and I were on the ground, searching frantically for something precious to our family that was now lost. We were panic stricken, crying at the prospect of never finding this item. My husband lay in his bed, unaffected and untouched by the pain that surrounded him.

I didn't want this. This was not my choice.
Where can I turn but to God.

The Lord is my strength and my shield;
my heart trusts in Him, and He helps me.
—Psalm 28:7

Father, in this extremely difficult time, help me remember
your promise.

"I will never leave you or forsake you."

50

It amazes me how God places people in your path. Being deeply depressed, I thought I needed to try yet again to go through the motions. I stopped by a local nail salon. I met a lady there that I knew and explained to her my current life situation. She gasped and put her hand to her heart. I knew from her reaction that she had felt the same pain and rejection from someone she loved. She sat with me and encouraged me.

I didn't want this rejection in my life. This was not my choice.
Where can I turn but to God.

I waited patiently for the Lord; He turned to me and heard my cry.
He lifted me out of the slimy pit, out of the mud and mire; He set
my feet on a rock and gave me a firm place to stand.
—Psalm 40:1–2

Father, in this extremely difficult time, help me remember
your promise.

"I will never leave you or forsake you."

I have cried every day since this began. It's surprising where you find yourself crying when you have been thrown away. I have cried in my car, in restaurants, at work, in the bathroom, in the shower, at the hair salon, on the back porch, in church, watching TV, on the phone, and just about anywhere else you can imagine. Most of all I cry in my bed. I am crying on the inside when I am smiling on the outside.

I didn't want this. This was not my choice.
Where can I turn but to God.

You keep track of all my sorrows. You have collected all my tears in your bottle.
You have recorded each one in your book.
—Psalm 56:8

Father, in this extremely difficult time, help me remember
your promise.

"I will never leave you or forsake you."

It has been nearly two weeks to the minute since my life drastically changed. I go to work as I always do. It is hard to go through the motions without crying. I am not the same person. I am empty.

I didn't want this. This was not my choice.
Where can I turn but to God.

Guide me into your truth. For you are the God who delivers me;
on you I rely all day long.
—Psalm 25:5

Father, in this extremely difficult time, help me remember
your promise.

"I will never leave you or forsake you."

Everyone has a story; everyone has difficulties. Some are brought on by life, and some are perpetrated by others. Both can be devastating. I spoke with a man this week who has had more than his share of challenges. His life has been consumed with physical and emotional pain. He told me that he felt he was in a tunnel. He could see a light in the far distance, and he was relying on that light to get him through. I listened to him for a long time. I felt his pain through his words. Without going into detail and with tears in my eyes, I shared that I was in a tunnel too. My tunnel was filled with despair and hopelessness, but in the distance I could barely recognize a pinpoint of light. I was not even sure it was light. I thought I could hear a voice, perhaps a whisper. I needed to hear what the voice was saying, but in my sorrow I could not understand the words. He looked at me for what seemed like a long moment, and then he simply said, "Kathiey, that's God."

I don't know what to do.
I didn't want to be in this tunnel. This was not my choice.
Where can I turn but to God.

After the earthquake came a fire, but the Lord was not in the fire.
And after the fire came a gentle whisper.
—1 Kings 19:12

Father, in this extremely difficult time, help me remember
your promise.

"I will never leave you or forsake you."

These days are my own personal hell. What a waste. We had a wonderful family. We had a beautiful home, Sunday dinners together, and the dream of family travel. We had the dog and the white picket fence. All of this was thrown away by the decision of one person.

I didn't ask for this. This was not my choice.
Where can I turn but to God.

Surely God is my help;
the Lord is the one who sustains me.
—Psalm 54:4

Father, in this extremely difficult time, help me remember
your promise.

"I will never leave you or forsake you."

During our ups and downs over the past thirty-seven years, I never saw this coming. He says he is not like his dad, but I think he is. Over the years he has often spoken of the pain he saw his mom endure because of his father's decisions. The same pain he is putting me through now. He spoke also of the pain his father inflicted on his family. The same pain he is putting our family through now.

I didn't ask for this. This was not my choice.
Where can I turn but to God.

For I know the plans I have for you, says the Lord. They are plans for
good and not for disaster, to give you a future and a hope.
—Jeremiah 29:11

Father, in this extremely difficult time, help me remember
your promise.

"I will never leave you or forsake you."

I forced myself out of the house. I went to a local garden to try to see the beauty of God's creation that surrounds me, even in the midst of my pain. I spent three hours in the garden. It was hard to place one foot in front of the other. I could feel my heart pounding, and at times I felt short of breath, as though I could easily faint. I knew that this fatigue was caused by my overpowering emotional distress. Yes, there was incredible beauty in the garden, but it was hard for me to see. My sorrow blinded me. Lord, help me to see the beauty that surrounds me, even in pain.

I didn't want this sorrow. This was not my choice.
Where can I turn but to God.

*I always remember that the Lord is with me. He is here
close by my side, so nothing can defeat me.*
—Psalm 16:8

Father, in this extremely difficult time, help me remember
your promise.

"I will never leave you or forsake you."

I sit outside on the new stone patio. There is new furniture and lovely landscaping, but no one to share it with. I am not feeling strong.

I didn't ask for this. This was not my choice.
Where can I turn but to God.

The Lord is close to the brokenhearted
and saves those who are crushed in spirit.
—Psalm 34:18

Father, in this extremely difficult time, help me remember
your promise.

"I will never leave you or forsake you."

It was another bad night. I couldn't sleep, and my mind was consumed with anxiety and worry. My skin crawled, and my head hurt. There was a hole in my heart. I began to lean on escape again. Somehow there is peace in the ability to run away—no more pain, no more disappointment, and no more destroyed dreams.

I didn't want this. This was not my choice.
Where can I turn but to God.

The Lord your God is in your midst, a mighty one who will save;
He will rejoice over you with gladness; He will quiet you by his love;
He will exult over you with loud singing.
—Zephaniah 3:17

Father, in this extremely difficult time, help me remember
your promise.

"I will never leave you or forsake you."

My husband was a pastor for nearly twenty years. You would think he would have learned from his own teachings not to hurt or damage others. I can't say when he decided his words from the pulpit were empty, at least in my case. There is nothing I can do about that.

I didn't ask for this. This was not my choice.
Where can I turn but to God.

But I will bless the person who puts his trust in me. He is like a tree growing near a stream and sending out roots to the water. It is not afraid when hot weather comes, because its leaves stay green; It has no worries when there is no rain; it keeps bearing fruit.
—Jeremiah 17:7–8

Father, in this extremely difficult time, help me remember
your promise.

"I will never leave you or forsake you."

Up again at 2:00 a.m. I am not sleeping. I am not eating. I am sinking deeper into depression. My friend told me that if you are sad for long periods of time, it changes the neurotransmitters in your brain, and you become clinically depressed. I believe that may be happening to me.

I didn't ask for this. This was not my choice.
Where can I turn but to God.

Therefore we do not despair, but even if our physical body is wearing away,
our inner person is being renewed day by day.
—2 Corinthians 4:16

Father, in this extremely difficult time, help me remember
your promise.

"I will never leave you or forsake you."

I am a nurse, and I spent many years working in the emergency room. Many times a patient who had gone through some type of trauma would appear so strong, so in control. That would work until someone the person cared for arrived at his or her bedside. Then the patient's guard would come down, and that person would crumble into the arms of the loved one. This happened to me. I have a wonderful brother. His name is Bruce, and he has Down's syndrome. We have been extremely close since we were kids. We talk on the phone often. Sometimes we sing songs together on the phone. Not lately. I have not felt strong enough to talk to him since my nightmare began. Today the phone rang, and it was Bruce. Thinking I was strong enough, I answered. As soon as he spoke, I began to sob. Through my tears I heard Bruce's voice. "Don't cry, Kathiey. You are my sister, and I love you. I will pray for you." I did not tell him why I was crying.

I didn't want this, Bruce. This was not my choice.
Where can I turn but to God.

Come to me, all you who are weary and burdened, and I will give you rest. Take my yoke upon you and learn from me, for I am gentle and humble in heart, and you will find rest for your souls.
—Matthew 11:28–29

Father, in this extremely difficult time, help me remember
your promise.

"I will never leave you or forsake you."

There is a house I drive by several times a week. It is a beautiful, rustic yet elegant home. There were always cars in the driveway—lots of people and activity. It seemed to be a happy place. During the Christmas holiday, this house was beautifully decorated with lights and several Christmas trees. It was a sight to behold. I have learned that this family was going through a divorce, and I have watched this house deteriorate—no more festive lights, no cars in the driveway. The place looks empty and unkempt. I noticed this week that there is a very large For Sale sign in the front yard. Before my current situation, I was saddened by the negative effect that divorce can have on a family. Now, of course, I am living it. Now I worry as I look at my own home. I don't know if I will get to stay here.

I didn't ask for this. This was not my choice.
Where can I turn but to God.

The Lord said I will guide you along the best pathway for your life.
I will advise you and watch over you.
—Psalm 32:8

Father, in this extremely difficult time, help me remember
your promise.

"I will never leave you or forsake you."

I realize now that I will have to hire an attorney. I also realize that what is left of my inheritance will fund my divorce. Money that could have been used for the good of my family will now go toward legal fees, all because of the choices of one person.

I didn't ask for this. This was not my choice.
Where can I turn but to God.

He will cover you with His wings; you will be safe in his care.
His faithfulness will protect and defend you.
—Psalm 91:4

Father, in this extremely difficult time, help me remember
your promise.

"I will never leave you or forsake you."

78

I met with a lady that was in my situation. She said that the pain was worse than death. I agreed with her and said, "It is like a death, but with intent." She thought for a second and said, "That would be murder." I said, "That is true. It is the deliberate murder of a family."

I didn't ask for this. This was not my choice.
Where can I turn but to God.

Be still and know that I am God.
—Psalm 46:10

Father, in this extremely difficult time, help me remember
your promise.

"I will never leave you or forsake you."

My story does not end here. I see this process as the beginning, the journey, and the joy. My first book, The Beginning, is about getting through the initial pain and trauma with the help of my faith and support of my friends. My second book will be about The Journey, the steps we need to take to reestablish our lives. My third will be about The Joy—that is the part I like best. And yes, there is or there will be joy. Please hang on through the pain and the journey. God has a plan for your life. Please don't give up like I nearly did. Reach out to your friends, and let God guide you.

It has been over three years since all this began for me, and I am finding joy—joy in my life as a single woman, joy in God and His Word, joy in my family and friendships, and joy in God's beauty that surrounds us, even in our pain.

God's Beauty

There is beauty that surrounds us even in our pain.
A tiny bit of sun and light cascading through the rain.
From where I sit I find it if I take the time to see.
A glimpse through tears God's beauty and its surrounding me.
KathieyV

Thoughts

Thoughts

Thoughts

Thoughts

Thoughts

Thoughts

Thoughts

Thoughts

Thoughts

Thoughts

Thoughts

Thoughts

Thoughts

Thoughts

Thoughts

Thoughts

Thoughts

Thoughts

_____
_____
_____
_____
_____
_____
_____
_____
_____
_____
_____
_____
_____
_____
_____
_____
_____
_____
_____
_____
_____

Made in the USA
Charleston, SC
10 February 2017